THE HOW AND WHY WONDER BOOK OF
PRIMITIVE MAN

Written by DONALD BARR
Assistant Dean, School of Engineering
Columbia University, New York

Illustrated by MATTHEW KALMENOFF

Editorial Production: DONALD D. WOLF

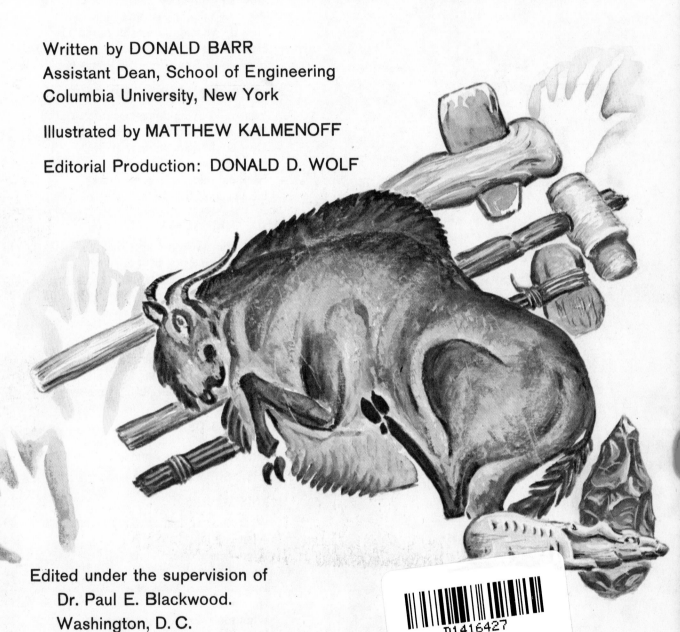

Edited under the supervision of
    Dr. Paul E. Blackwood.
    Washington, D. C.

Text and illustrations approved by
    Oakes A. White, Brooklyn Children's Museum, Brooklyn, New York

GROSSET & DUNLAP • **Publishers** • **NEW YORK**

Introduction

This *How and Why Wonder Book* deals with a question that is perplexing and fascinating — "Where did man come from?" The book relates how scientists use the records of "prehistory" to help answer this question. It throws light on various theories about how man developed from primitive beginnings to a creature who first used simple tools and then more complex ones. It reminds us that after thousands of years, man began speaking and writing and, with these skills, history had begun.

The How and Why Wonder Book of Primitive Man reveals how different kinds of scientists — archaeologists, anthropologists, geologists and others — combine their discoveries and knowledge to fill in the gaps with information that is needed to get a clearer picture of early man. We learn, too, how it is that there are people of many different kinds and appearances in the world today. Yet we see, also, that men everywhere probably have a common ancestry and that all men are "brothers under the skin." At no other time in history has it been so important for people everywhere to possess attitudes favorable to understanding each other.

This book can help parents, teachers and children to build sound knowledge by supplying up-to-date information on common questions about man's origins.

Paul E. Blackwood

Dr. Blackwood is a professional employee in the U. S. Office of Education. This book was edited by him in his private capacity and no official support or endorsement by the Office of Education is intended or should be inferred.

Library of Congress Catalog Card Number: 61-12935

ISBN: 0-448-05024-2 (WONDER EDITION)
ISBN: 0-448-04022-0 (TRADE EDITION)
ISBN: 0-448-03832-3 (LIBRARY EDITION)

Contents

Early man developed the use of fire, which made him master of the animal kingdom.

fury and it charged them, trumpeting. Then they ran before it. Screeching figures like big featherless birds they were. They dodged this way and that and led the mastodon on and on. And then . . . it stepped on what had looked like ordinary leaves and twigs, yet the ground gave way under it. And there was a deep pit underneath the leaves, and it crashed down, and in a moment the vicious ani-mals were upon the mastodon, slashing at it with tree branches that had sharp stones growing on them, and the victim was dead.

Here is one of the Invaders, squatting on the pebbly edge of the river. His heavy, almost hairless shoulders are hunched forward; his tangled head is cocked downward watchfully; his hand clutches a stout, sharp twig. There is no sound except the gurgle of the stream dashing and whirling between the

The New Animal

There was a new kind of animal in the forest . . .

The wild dogs found a strange scent and followed it through the thick bushes and along the pebbly banks of the rivers, until, in the cold of the night, they came to an open hillside. And there, crouching in the hollow under a hanging cliff, were the Invaders. They were like no other animals the dogs had ever seen, and there were many of them in the pack, and their strong smell excited the dogs, standing back among the trees, fur bristling and mouths dripping. The new animals would make a good fight and a good feast! But in the midst of the Invader pack there was . . . Something Else. It was just as if a little puddle of daylight had been left behind when the night fell. And in the center of that light-puddle was a snapping, dancing thing. It was the color of the sun and hot like the sun — Fire. So the dogs turned and ran back into the dark woods. Only when they were alone with their hunger under the sheltering leaves did they lift up their muzzles and howl.

The next day, a saber-toothed tiger watched the Invaders coming through the trees. How noisy they were, these new animals! They made loud grunting and chattering sounds with their mouths, and they tore their way recklessly through the bushes, as if there were no other animals in the forest. They walked in a clumsy way, straining up on their hind legs. Their strange, flat, front paws seemed to be of no use in walking, and just hung down or pushed aside the branches. The creatures seemed to have almost no claws at all. They had long dirty manes, but the rest of their fur was poor and thin. However, they were biggish animals and bulged with meat, and the tiger thought that if it charged them suddenly, the whole foolish, brawling herd would run away in fright, and it could feast on the first one that fell. So the tiger chose its prey — a female carrying her cub. Its great mouth yawned open in a snarl of joy, its long, curving upper teeth flashed, and it leaped. But it was a bad leap. The tiger's claws only raked the creature's flesh, and she gave a high scream. And instead of plunging into the bushes to escape, the whole herd turned to their wounded member. It was then that the tiger saw The Claw. One of the Invaders raised his front paw as he ran, and now it looked weak and useless no longer, for the tiger saw there was a strange, straight, gray toe growing from it — long and terrible — and The Claw buried itself in the tiger's throat, and the tiger died.

Even the mastodon, with its fearsome tusks and its curling powerful trunk that could pull up a young tree, was helpless before the Invaders. A little band of the new animals found a bull mastodon in the forest. A great lord of the herd it was — all the animals of the forest walked softly when it was near. But these creatures picked up rocks and pieces of trees in their strange clever forepaws and threw them at the mastodon so that its little eyes reddened with

stones. There is no movement except the flash of the sunlight on the water and the glitter of the creature's eyes as they peer this way and that into the speckled depths . . . A streak of movement! The creature's hand shoots out, and a fish is pinned to the bottom of the stream by the stick. The creature seizes the squirming fish with his other hand, pulls it out — and begins to eat it.

He stands up. Look at him. He is an ugly fellow. He stands only a little over five feet tall, but the upper part of his body is large. His neck is thick. His shoulders slump forward heavily. His matted chest bulges out in a great curve. His arms are fairly long, but they look longer because his legs are thick and bowed and very short, and he seems to be keeping his knees slightly bent. Under the shaggy hair, his head is large, but you have to look carefully to see this, because he has a way of pushing his face forward so that the back of his head sinks down between his shoulders. He has a big face. He has immense brow-ridges jutting out above his suspicious eyes. His forehead is very low and sloping. He has an enormous jaw — which he grinds forward and backward in a strange way as he chews the fish — but he has almost no chin.

Look hard at him. He is the new master of the forest. There is no animal he cannot kill. With these strange, clever front paws of his — his hands — he is going to sew and knot together their skins to provide warmth and shelter for himself, partly defeating even the greatest and oldest of his enemies, the cold and the storm. With the powerful brain behind that low forehead, this animal is going to change other animals, making them serve and obey him. This forest where he now stands spitting out fish bones and peering into the shadows for his enemies, this vast forest will be cut down, and in its place he will build a great city. That brain of his will perhaps think of fantastic crimes, things too bloody for a saber-toothed tiger, but that brain of his will also think of fantastic beauty, of sounds that will make your heart race in your chest, of shapes and colors that will stop the breath in your nostrils . . .

He still has such a long way to go! But he has come far already. He himself does not know how far. No one in the Invader band remembers when they started, or where. Always they have been on the move. They hunt in a place until there are no more deer or dogs or horses, and they gather berries and nuts until the branches are bare, and then they start out again through the forests. Their mothers and fathers before them were wanderers all their lives — from hill to hill, from river to river, from winter cave to winter cave.

This is a brave band. It has gone up to the very edge of the Cold, to where almost all the trees are dead and none of the other animals will go, except the reindeer. Some of the bravest have even seen the Moving Mountain itself. This one saw it. It is a great wall of ice reaching up and up into a sky that is filled with snow, and when he listened he could hear the mountain crawling along the ground, making terrible noises as if the earth were groaning with pain. It crawled too slowly to see, but on the cruel white face of the mountain he could see where it had picked up huge stones and trees and devoured them.

The old ones in the band tell stories at the campfire. They tell of other kinds of places — of lands where it is always summer, of lands where there are strange beasts almost like themselves but living in trees, of rivers so wide that no one can see the other side, and of lands of death where there is no water and no grass. These places are many winters away, many lives away. But the band has been there . . .

The stories of the old ones are true, and so are many stories the oldest of the old don't know. For this creature is a Man, and the story of Man is so long that no one could tell it all, and so astonishing that no one would believe it all. That story began with dust out in the freezing space between the stars. It took place in the boiling rock of the volcanoes, in great clouds of gas and great lightning-storms that lasted millions of years, in the slime at the bottom of oceans, in mud, in treetops. It took place in bits of strange chemicals too small to see, and in murderous giant lizards. We ourselves know only a little of the story, and most of what we know we have had to guess, using the brain we have inherited from that strange creature in the forest . . .

And so the new animal, the Man, finishes eating his fish, spits out a bit of fin, and lumbers off to his lair.

Before History

About fifty centuries ago, writing was

What does "prehistoric" mean?

invented so people could put things down on clay or stone or animal skin or paper if they thought it might be important to remember them. Anything that is important to people is a part of history. So we may say that written history is about 5,000 years old.

But there have been people — people who were more or less human — on the earth for about 500,000 years. So ninety-nine percent of the time that human beings have been on this planet was *before written history,* and that earlier time we call "prehistoric." "Pre" is just Latin for "before."

Scientists think that man's wonderful

When did prehistory start?

story really begins long before there were any men.

Man arrived on earth very late, and he probably didn't come suddenly. It seems quite clear that he slowly developed — we say that he "evolved" — from a much more primitive form, perhaps even from a very different kind of creature. In other words, your ancestors thousands, perhaps millions of years ago looked and acted very different from you. But every once in a while there were some children who were a little different from their parents, a little smarter or taller or less hairy. And these tiny improvements kept up over thousands and thousands of years until you came along.

Some people even believe that those old ancestors of yours may even have evolved in that same way from another kind of animal, and that kind from another, and that from another, and that from another. But this knowledge is still hidden, farther back into prehistory than we can see yet. Perhaps if we could only find enough facts, we could carry man's history all the way back to when the earth itself was formed, about 4,500,000,000 years ago!

Although there are no written records

How do we find out about prehistory?

that come to us from before the year 3000 B.C., there are other kinds of records. They do not use words but they tell us a lot.

Big events are not neat. In a war, for instance, the general's mother does not come and tidy up the battlefield afterward. So bullets or arrows are left around, and long, long afterward an expert on bullets or arrows may find one and say, "Ah! This bullet is the kind used in such-and-such a gun. And that gun was the kind used by such-and-such an army at such-and-such a time. Now, what was *that* army doing here?" And if he finds some bullets used by the other side in the battle, he may begin to figure out what happened in the war. And yet there might be no written records of that battle at all.

Or perhaps a tribe of Indians decides to move to a new hunting ground. They bundle up their belongings, roll up their tents, load their horses and set out. But of course they leave a lot of junk behind — worn-out things, or stuff too heavy to carry. And many years later an expert on Indians may come and say, "Ah! Such-and-such Indians once lived here. Here is a blanket with their design. We never knew *they* came this far south."

Graves are very important. Even if there are no gravestones, even if there are no clothes or favorite possessions buried with the dead, even if there is nothing but just bones, an expert on skeletons can learn a great deal. He can probably tell how long ago the people lived. He can tell how old each person was when he died. He might say, "Ah! These people lived around 3700 B.C. But see how this skull was cut open and grew back again — they must have known how to do some brain surgery even *then*!"

Such records are not complete. Often they are like puzzles that scientists must guess and argue about.

PROTEROZOIC ARCHEOZOIC	PALEOZOIC 340 MILLION YEARS							
1,500 MILLION YEARS	CAMBRIAN 90 MILLION YEARS	ORDOVICIAN 75 MILLION YEARS	SILURIAN 35 MILLION YEARS	DEVONIAN 65 MILLION YEARS	CARBONIFEROUS 50 MILLION YEARS	PERMIAN 25 MILLION YEARS	TRIASSIC 45 MILLION YEARS
ONLY FEW FOSSILS FOUND	INVERTEBRATES		FISHES		AMPHIBIANS		

Dozens of different kinds of scientists can tell us things about prehistoric times. When we want to know about how the earth formed, we go to the *astronomers* (Greek for "star-lawyers"), who study stars and planets; and we go to the *physicists* (Greek for "nature-followers"), who study the forces and particles that form the atom; and we go to the *chemists* (Greek for "juice-pourers"), who study how atoms behave. Of course, they have no records at all of what happened 4,500,000,000 years

Who are the experts on prehistory?

Early man used primitive but deadly weapons as he hunted the mastodon, an ancestor of the elephant.

There is something wrong with this picture. A dinosaur could not have chased a man, for as we know, dinosaurs were already extinct when man emerged.

The chart is a record of life on earth as told in its rocks. It is divided into eras, which are divided into periods, and shows the form of life dominant in each phase of the earth's geological history. You can see how late is man's appearance on the earth. All figures in the chart signify duration of time.

SOZOIC		CENOZOIC	
MILLION YEARS		70 MILLION YEARS	
RASSIC MILLION YEARS	CRETACEOUS 60 MILLION YEARS	PALEOCENE to PLEISTOCENE 70 MILLION YEARS	RECENT

INOSAURS   MAMMALS   MAN

ago. But from studying how things work now, they can tell us how things might have worked then.

If we want to know when things happened on earth, and what the earth was like when different animals were evolving, we go to the *geologists* (Greek for "talkers about the earth"), who study rocks and soils.

When we want to know what animals evolved, we go to the *paleontologists* (Greek for "talkers about ancient beings"), who study the buried bones and tracks of animals of the past. And when we want to know how animals evolved, we go to the *geneticists* (Greek for "birth-followers"), who are trying to find out why we are like our parents and sometimes not quite like them.

When we want to know about human bones, we go to the *physical anthropologists* (Greek for "talkers about what man is made of"), who learn about the human body. When we want to know about the tools and ornaments that belonged to prehistoric men, we go to the *archeologists* (Greek for "talkers about ancient things"), who study all the objects made and used by people in past ages.

For instance, you will often see cartoons showing cave men being chased by dinosaurs. But this could never have happened. The physical anthropologists tell us which bones are the bones of the prehistoric men who lived in caves. The paleontologists tell us which bones are the bones of the giant reptiles. The geologists tell us that the human bones come from layers of earth that are 50,000 years old, and the dinosaur bones come from rocks 150,000,000 years old.

Almost all the bones, tools, weapons and ornaments that tell us what men were like and how they lived in the distant past are buried in the ground. Many have been found by accident. But most of the records of the past still lie beneath the surface of the earth, waiting to be discovered.

How do we find the records of the past?

Fortunately for science, man is a messy animal. In the last hundred years or so, some people in some places have learned that dirt breeds germs and germs cause disease — so they have gone in for cleanliness and garbage disposal. But the old way of doing things was just to throw rubbish away and leave it. When a prehistoric man finished gnawing on a bone, he tossed it on the ground. When he killed a handsome animal and scraped down its skin to make a new suit for himself, he dropped the old skin — it became

How do the records of the past get buried?

BATON

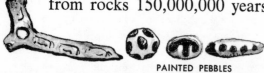

PAINTED PEBBLES

A cave belonging to primitive man, still containing pottery and other utensils, was discovered in the Middle East not so long ago. A cross section of the earth under the cave shows layer upon layer of refuse dating back to many generations.

a rug or a bed. When he broke a stone tool, he kicked the pieces out of the way. When he died, he might well have been rolled onto the trash heap with the other old bones.

Wherever man lived in caves, the floor was covered with stinking trash. People trampled it into the dirt and tracked mud over it, and as layer after layer of this refuse was added, the cave floor slowly rose. The tribe would leave. The cave would be empty, or bears would live in it. The garbage on the floor would rot away until only bones and stone chips were buried in black dirt. A new tribe would come and a new layer would start. Scientists have dug out caves where these floor layers went down sixty feet.

Where men lived outdoors, or in lean-tos made of tree branches and animal hides, rains and floods would wash sand and gravel over the old campsites, or landslides would bury them. Roving bands of prehistoric men were slaughtered by enemies, and their bodies were left for the animals, and the leaf-mold

and forest growth slowly covered the bones. Villages and even cities were abandoned, or burned, or sacked, and new towns were built on the leveled ruins. When Heinrich Schliemann dug up the city of Troy, he found nine Troys, one above the other.

The whole record of life, long before man, is kept in the same way. As thousands of thousands of years have passed since life first began on this planet, vast, slow surges in the earth's molten core have shifted the rocky crust of the world. Continents rose from the oceans. Great seas swirled into the collapsing plains. Lakes dried up. Rivers cut deep canyons in the soil and stone. In these changes, life and death went on. Wherever water has laid down beds of soil or sand or gravel or rock formed from hardened mud, scientists can dig down and go back in time — the topmost layers which record the Age of Man, and then down into ancient layers where the bones and shells of strange animals that vanished millions of years ago silently tell their story.

11

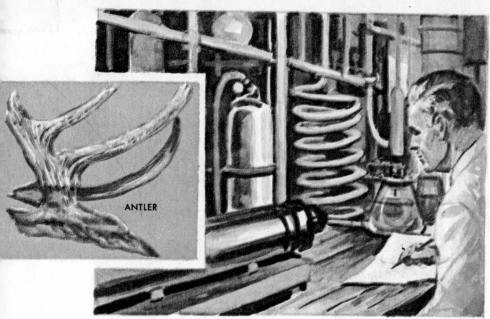

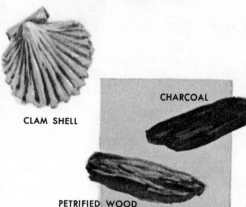

FOLSOM POINT

ANTLER

CLAM SHELL

CHARCOAL

PETRIFIED WOOD

A scientist applies the carbon-14 test to an antler to determine its age.

How do we know how old things are? In reading the long story told to us by the traces that living creatures have left in the earth, it is usually not hard to tell which plants or animals lived before or after others. As we go down into a series of layers of rock, or gravel, or packed mud, we know that the deeper the layer, the older it is. In many parts of the world, there are series of layers that are very much alike. The same little shells or animal bones are embedded in layers of the same kind of rock or earth. Many of these are kinds of animals that died out after a while. So we can guess that a certain layer in America was laid down at the same time as a certain layer in Europe. And slowly we can build up a kind of list, in the proper order, of all the things that took place in each part of the world for millions of years — the floods and droughts, the kinds of animals, the kinds of men.

But even when we know the order in which things happened, it is hard to tell just how long ago they happened. Until a few years ago, scientists really had to guess how long it took rocks to form or mud to pile up. But now they have invented some strange and ingenious ways of finding the "dates" of ancient layers of the records of the past.

Several new methods of "dating" depend on tiny clocks hidden inside the atoms of certain substances. For instance, practically all the chemicals that living things are made of contain a certain kind of atom called the carbon atom. And there is one form of carbon atom that is special: it is a little heavier than the ordinary carbon atom, and it is "radioactive" — that is, it falls apart by itself after a while and turns into another kind of atom. This kind of carbon is called carbon-14, and it falls apart at a steady rate which never changes. If there were 10,000 atoms of regular carbon and 100 atoms of carbon-14 in a certain piece of bone in 3600 B.C., then there are 10,000 atoms of regular carbon and only 50 atoms of carbon-14 in that piece of bone today.

CROSS SECTION THROUGH LAYERS OF ROCK

DINOSAUR FOOTPRINTS

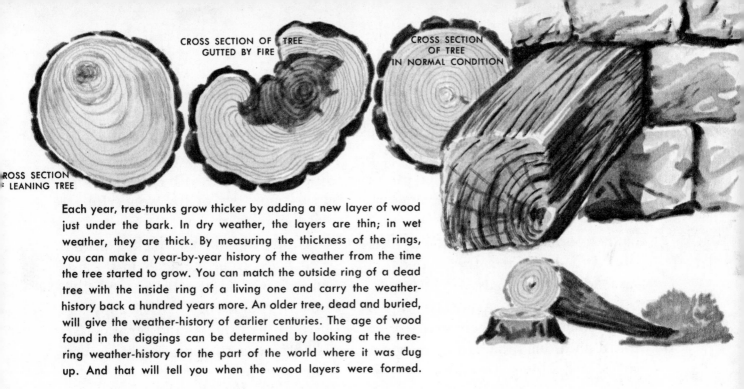

CROSS SECTION OF TREE GUTTED BY FIRE

CROSS SECTION OF TREE IN NORMAL CONDITION

CROSS SECTION OF LEANING TREE

Each year, tree-trunks grow thicker by adding a new layer of wood just under the bark. In dry weather, the layers are thin; in wet weather, they are thick. By measuring the thickness of the rings, you can make a year-by-year history of the weather from the time the tree started to grow. You can match the outside ring of a dead tree with the inside ring of a living one and carry the weather-history back a hundred years more. An older tree, dead and buried, will give the weather-history of earlier centuries. The age of wood found in the diggings can be determined by looking at the tree-ring weather-history for the part of the world where it was dug up. And that will tell you when the wood layers were formed.

Now it happens that carbon-14 atoms only get into animals, along with regular carbon atoms, while the animals are alive. So scientists have invented wonderful ways of counting these tiny atoms — so tiny they cannot be seen even with the most powerful microscope — and comparing the different kinds of carbon atoms to figure out how long ago the animal died. In great laboratories filled with gleaming tangles of glass tubing and flashing lights and the whir and click of the atom-counters, scientists can test a little crumb of bone and say:

"This man died 75,000 years ago."

Where Did Man Come From?

The story of the earth began in the terrible cold of empty space. This is how many scientists think it happened — or *could* have happened: Where our sun and the earth and the other planets now are, there was once only a vast dark cloud of dust and gas. Slowly, gently, the light from the stars around it pushed this material together. Then the pull of gravity squeezed it together harder and

Where did living things come from?

harder and harder. In the center, a lump formed, and its gravity pulled more and more material in, and finally it got so big that the atoms in the center of it were squashed by the tremendous weight of the material around them. This started a wild flare-up of nuclear energy, like an endless hydrogen bomb explosion, and soon the lump was a huge glowing ball — the sun.

Around it the rest of the dust cloud wheeled and swirled, and little whirlpools of dust began to form, and they too became lumps, and these formed glowing hot planets and their moons.

When the third planet from the sun — the one we call Earth — cooled a little, it had a soft wrapping of air around it, but not the air we breathe. If you had tried to breathe the air of the newborn earth, you would have choked to death in a few seconds. It was made of certain gases — hydrogen, methane, ammonia and water vapor. For millions of years, there were terrific storms all around the earth, and great flashes of lightning sizzled through the clouds. And for millions of years, the sun's rays beat down. The electricity and the rays rearranged the atoms of the gases into strange acids called "amino acids," which are the building blocks that your flesh and blood are made of. Here and there, the floating amino acids combined into the right arrangements, and tiny bits of "protein" were formed. Protein is not quite alive.

And at last some other acids, even more wonderful, were formed. They were "nucleic acids," and when these atom-groups, or molecules, were linked together in a certain way, other acid stuff stuck to them *and arranged itself next to them in the same pattern.* These were the first living things.

What is evolution? All living creatures are members of the same great family. That idea is called "the theory of evolution." The lion, the giraffe, the worm, the eagle, the sparrow and the wasp are all cousins. Scientists believe that their first ancestor was one "cell," floating in the stormy oceans of the earth two billion years ago. It was a tiny cluster of proteins with a special corkscrew-shaped set of the wonderful nucleic acids in the middle of it. This middle part of the cell picked up bits of chemical from the acids in the protein-sack around it, and arranged them into a copy of itself. Then the copy split off from the original and separated. It pulled part of the protein cluster with it and became the center of a new cell. Then both cells split. So there were four cells. Then eight. Then sixteen. And soon there were billions of cells, each containing a perfect copy of the nucleic-acid corkscrew.

Gradually these cells began to change. They became specialists. Some specialized in producing one kind of chemical, others produced other kinds. Some changed shape when an electric current touched them. Others were electrified when light hit them. And these specialist-cells no longer lived by themselves. They lived in groups or colonies, and divided the different kinds of work between them.

These colonies copied themselves, too. But it was not as if a football team went out and organized another football team, with the quarterback picking the new quarterback and the left tackle picking the new left tackle. It was rather as if there were a master plan for the colony, written down in nucleic

AMOEBA

JELLYFISH

AMPHIOXUS

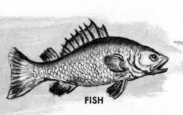

FISH

FROG

acids. Each cell had a copy. And a copy was kept in a special cell to give to the new colony.

Then the master plans changed little by little, and the colonies became more and more complicated. The cells that were sensitive to light began to be the eyes of the colony. The cells that gave off electricity were the nerves. Some of the chemical work-cells were the stomach. And now there were animals.

As soon as scientists — these were the geneticists, the "birth - followers" —discovered that each animal had a master plan that was passed on from animal to animal, they had a big problem to solve. If the designs were just copied over and over, how could the animals ever change?

How do different animals evolve?

After all, their friends the paleontologists—the "talkers about ancient beings" — could show them plenty of animal skeletons which proved that there *had* been changes. Animals had gotten bigger, or gotten smaller, or changed shape.

If an animal had a father and a mother, its design would be a sort of mixture of its parents — and sometimes a bit of its grandparents, too. That would explain how one horse might be different from another horse. But it would not explain how, in a few million years, all the horses lost their toes and got hoofs.

Changes in the plan of an animal are called "mutations"—which is just Latin for "change." And scientists say that little accidents are happening all the time to the acids of the master plan. For instance, there are rays from outer space that are always shooting through us. Parts of the acid-stuff might get shifted around by these "cosmic rays." Mostly these accidents just spoil the copy of the plan so badly that it cannot be used, but once in a while an accident makes a change that can really work.

And what you are is a collection of millions and millions of such changes, in the form of a colony of fifty trillion cells.

Not all changes are good. If a mutation is extremely different, then the little creature may not live long enough to be born. But new and different offspring are always being born in the great family of living creatures—among men as well as among other living things.

What is natural selection?

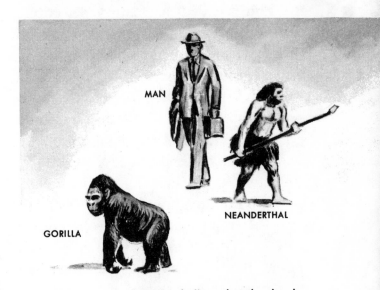

MAN

NEANDERTHAL

GORILLA

MULE DEER

Scientists believe that the development of life on earth began with one-celled animals. After two billion years, man emerged.

LIZARD

SWALLOW

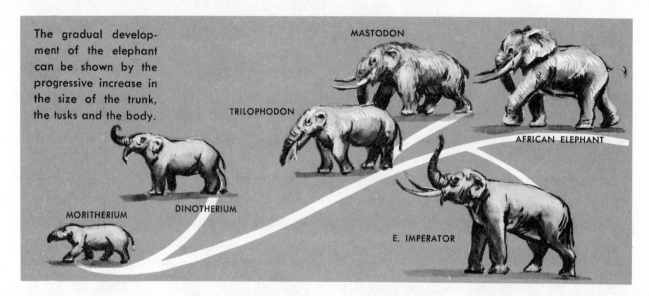

The gradual development of the elephant can be shown by the progressive increase in the size of the trunk, the tusks and the body.

MASTODON

TRILOPHODON

AFRICAN ELEPHANT

MORITHERIUM

DINOTHERIUM

E. IMPERATOR

If the mutation makes the animal weaker, it is more likely to get killed in a fight, or to die of sickness or hunger. It will not live as long and have as many children as its ordinary brothers. So the old plan will be carried on and the new one will die out.

If the mutation makes the animal stronger or more clever, it will win its fights and eat well, and the animal will probably live long and have many children to carry on the new master plan.

This is called the "natural selection" of mutations, and it means that the master plan of animals is always slowly changing to fit the world they have to live in. For example, drugs such as penicillin used to be wonderful at killing germs, including the terrible staphylococcus microbes that cause infections. Doctors gave penicillin to practically everybody for practically everything. So the staphylococcus microbe had to live in a world full of penicillin. And now many staphylococcus microbes have a mutation that keeps them unharmed by penicillin.

The same thing seems to have been happening to men. That is why you have longer legs than the fellow we met in the forest in the first chapter.

There used to be a great argument among scientists about how giraffes got their long necks. For the skeletons of ancient giraffes showed that once upon a time they had short necks. And this is an important question. Because you got your excellent brain the same way the giraffe got its long neck.

How did the giraffe get its neck?

Some scientists claimed the giraffes had lived by eating the leaves off the trees and after a while, when they had eaten all the leaves from the lower branches, they had to stretch their necks to get at their food. They stretched so hard that their necks grew a little longer, and their children were born with longer necks, which they stretched still more. So *their* children were born with still longer necks, and so on and so on. In other words, these scientists said that if your body changes, the same change will take place in your master plan.

Other scientists said this was nonsense. They said that nothing that happened to your body would make any change in your master plan. The giraffes ate all the leaves off the lower branches. But some giraffe-families happened to be born with longer necks than others, just as in some people-families everyone has a longer nose than in some other families. This had nothing to do with stretching. It was because of little shifts in the acids of the master plan. However, the giraffe-families that did have longer necks got more to eat. They were healthier and had a better chance to get away from lions and other giraffe-eaters. So the long-neck families had more children than the short-neck families. The long-neck mutations won because they were better tree-eaters and there were not quite enough trees to go around.

They were right. These scientists, led by the great naturalist, Charles Darwin, said that *man evolved because his powerful brain helped him to stay alive.*

When Darwin's books on evolution

Do all people believe the theory of evolution?

were printed a hundred years ago, many people said Darwin did not believe in God's plan, but in a horrible universe run by lucky accidents and greedy fighting. They said he was making man out to be nothing more than a smart ape. But these people need not have worried. The theory of evolution says certain things happened. It does not say, and it could not say, *why* those things happened. If God made the world and runs the world, then evolution *is* God's plan. And it is a majestic and beautiful plan. With evolution, even accidents are part of the plan of life, and even the lowest creature is part of the family life. The theory of evolution does not say man is only a smarter kind of ape. It says that for two billion years living forms were tried and improved and tried and improved in preparation for the arrival of man as we know him upon the scene of life upon the earth.

And Then...Man!

A hundred years ago, all educated men

Were our ancestors apes?

were talking excitedly about the new theories of evolution. Very few of them took the trouble to read the books written by Darwin and his friends, however, and so a lot of silly ideas got started by men who thought they could get knowledge without studying. Some of these ideas were invented by people who were so sure Darwin was wicked that they made up wicked ideas and said they were Darwin's. Others were invented by people who said they were supporting Darwin, but who really meant that they wanted Darwin to support them and their own pet theories. Then the less educated people got hold of these ideas and thought that this was what the new sci-

though no one really knows for sure, that man and the anthropoid apes may have had a common ancestor millions of years ago, and far back along the stream of evolution. If so, it is quite certain that such a common ancestor was not an "ape," a chimpanzee or a gorilla, like the ones we see in zoos today.

Maybe the animals that were the ancestors of both apes and men — "the missing link" as some people call them

Shown are side and top views of the skulls of a gorilla, a Neanderthal man and also modern man.

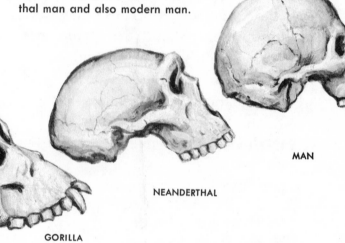

MAN

NEANDERTHAL

GORILLA

ence was all about. And it is surprising how many of those ideas are still going around today.

One of these is the idea that some of the apes you can see in a zoo — the gorillas or the chimpanzees or the orangutans — are exactly like our ancestors and look like and act like they must have. Some people seem to think that one set of chimps climbed down from a tree and evolved for a million years while the rest of the chimps stayed exactly the same for a million years. This is too hard to believe.

It is somewhat easier to believe, al-

— lived so long ago that they did not look anything like apes or men. Perhaps they had not even evolved as far as monkeys. Perhaps they looked like the tarsier, a funny animal from Asia, the size of a kitten, with huge eyes. In other words, perhaps men and apes evolved side by side but quite separately from each other for many, many millions of years.

Or maybe the animals that were the ancestors of both apes and men lived

more recently. In that case, they probably looked somewhat more like today's apes than like today's men. In other words, since the branches of the family tree parted, the apes have been evolving more slowly than we have.

Remember, after all, that our friend in the forest in the first chapter looked a little bit apelike himself.

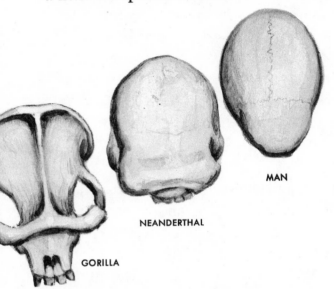

MAN

NEANDERTHAL

GORILLA

We cannot say when the first human beings appeared. There are three reasons for that. First, it is hard to say what "human" means. As far as we can tell from the bones we find, our ancestors first became "human" below the neck, and the brain followed later. But it is not walking upright, or having less body-hair, or having clumsy feet that makes us what we are. It is man's mind that makes him different from all other creatures, so we ought to say that the first true men were the first ones to have this peculiar brainpower.

When did the first men appear?

Second, skeletons do not have brains. They have empty spaces where the brains used to be. We can measure these spaces. But the size of a man's head does not tell how intelligent he is. For people with small heads or big heads can be either smart or stupid. Still, since we cannot do anything else, we measure the prehistoric skulls we find and hope the numbers mean something.

Third, we have not even found enough skulls yet. What we find of these *maybe*-human creatures is often just a jawbone, or even just a tooth, and the physical anthropologists have to guess what the head was like.

All we can honestly say is this: So far we have not found anything that looks very human that is older than the beginning of the great Ice Age.

About half a million years ago—some scientists say more and many scientists say less—the weather over the whole northern half of the earth began to change. The winters became colder. Rain and snow fell more

What was the Ice Age?

An iceberg breaks off from a glacier in the Ice Age.

19

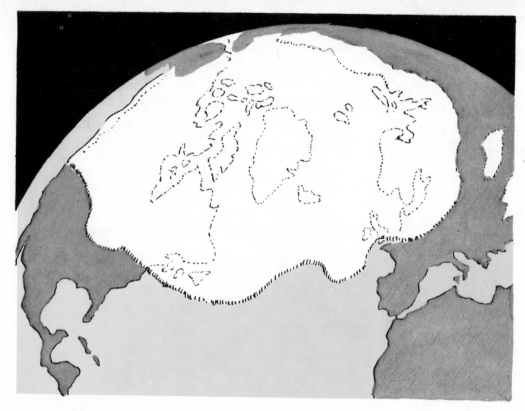

In the Ice Age, woolly rhinos were prevalent.

The map shows the extent of ice covering the world in the Ice Age.

and more of the time. In the mountainous places and up north, snow fell right through the summer. Up in the Arctic, the sheets of ice that covered land and sea grew thicker and slowly began to spread.

As wet air blew over the edge of this ice, snow kept falling and piled higher and higher, caking hard, until the edge of the great ice-sheet was a mile high. And as it inched southward, it picked up trees and great rocks. It swept the loose stones and soil before it, like a bulldozer as big as a continent. It crushed everything in its path. It pulled down mountainsides over the caves where our ancestors might have been living, and it splintered their bones in the burial grounds. Down into Europe and North America it came, grinding away the face of the earth, driving the animals before it.

This happened only in the northern hemisphere, but the amount of water there is in the world—in the seas and

rivers and lakes and in the clouds—does not change. So, as more water was frozen into the gigantic icecap, rivers and lakes dried and the level of the oceans dropped all over the globe. Islands and continents were joined together by bridges of dry land. Everywhere animals were on the move, going to live in places far from where they had evolved, and the kinds of mutations that worked well were different from the ones that worked well before.

Southward went the deer, the saber-tooth tiger, the horse. Down from the edge of the Arctic, retreating before the moving mountain of ice, came the cold-weather animals, the reindeer and the mammoth. (The last mammoths died thousands of years ago — perhaps killed off by that fierce new animal, man — yet living men have seen these great elephant-like beasts, covered with red-brown hair, as complete as if they had just died yesterday, with their last meals of grass and buttercups and fir tree branches still in their stomachs. For they were caught by the ice—falling into cracks in the glacier, or buried under avalanches—and preserved as if they had been kept in a deep-freeze. As the glacier melted, icebergs broke off and floated away northward, depositing the beasts, still frozen in huge blocks of ice and frozen mud, back in the Arctic wastelands.)

Down among the Alps in Switzerland, the ice on the mountain tops also spread, and there were times when the middle of Europe was almost cut off from the rest of the world by gigantic walls of ice. The animals caught inside this area changed—or died.

Then after thousands of years, the glaciers started to melt. Water poured down the slopes and rushed along the old river beds. The air became warmer. Inch by inch the ice retreated. The oceans and lakes began to fill again. The sun shone warmly the year round. In places where reindeer and perhaps a few manlike creatures had once shivered in the endless winter, animals from Africa now roamed. This was the "interglacial" period.

Then, thousands of years later, the glaciers came down again, and retreated, and again there was a long, sunny interglacial time when lions and hippopotamuses roamed over Europe.

Four times the ice came and four times it melted away. The last glacier retreat was only about 10,000 or 15,000 years ago. But of course . . . we do not know if it was really the last.

It was in this time of ten-thousand-year-ago summers and ten-thousand-year-ago winters that man came.

Ape-men or man-apes? In 1925, a professor in South Africa found the broken skull of a six-year-old in a layer of earth that seemed to have been formed about the same time that the glaciers were beginning at the other end of the world. The little fellow looked something like a young ape but looked human too, and the newspapers said it was "the missing link." Scientists decided it was probably a very stupid little creature, and so they called it a manlike ape.

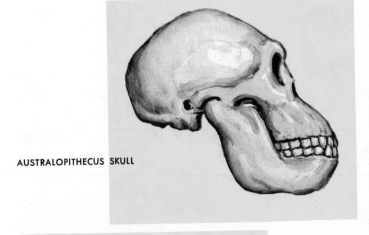

AUSTRALOPITHECUS SKULL

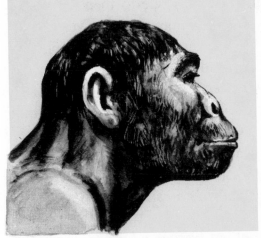

Australopithecus was a manlike ape that evolved in the south of Africa over one million years ago.

Since that discovery, many bones of grownups of the same sort have been dug up in southern Africa. Some seem to be from earlier times and some from later times. Some seem to be more man-like than others. Now no one is sure what to make of them. They have a name, though, *australopithecines* — Latin for "southern ape-like ones."

They could be just another kind of ape that happened to look more human than most and happened to die out. But not many people think so.

Or they could be our ancestors, just at the stage of evolution after they had become different from the apes' ancestors, but before they had gotten *very* different. The professors who discovered the creatures think so.

Or there might have been a time when *two* great races of intelligent beings were growing up on the planet. Perhaps the *australopithecines* had made an early start toward becoming the leaders of the family of life, but were not quite good enough. Or perhaps they had a late start and were on their way to becoming even better than men when some disaster came to them.

One thing about them is very mysterious. In several places, stone tools have been found with the bones of the *australopithecines*. Were they the creatures' own tools? Could such ape-like animals have done such human work? Or were they men's weapons? Did our ancestors, prowling the world during the Ice Age, sweep down and slaughter them?

The oldest bones that we are fairly sure belong to men whose descendants are still alive were found seventy years ago on the East Indian island of

What is pithecanthropus erectus?

Java. The so-called Java Man had a curious career. He got his name before he was even discovered. His discoverer first decided where he ought to be and went straight there and found him — and then decided he was not very important after all. But he is very important indeed.

A hundred years ago, when Darwin's theories were being argued about, everyone agreed that if evolution was true there must have been a point when our ancestors were exactly halfway between apes and men. This is not quite so, but one scientist was so confident that he gave a name to the missing creature — *pithecanthropus erectus*, which is Latin for "ape-man who stands upright."

A young Dutch doctor named Dubois decided that the place to look for this fellow was along the banks of a certain river in the East Indies, because human remains seemed to last well there and the geologists said the river bank was about the right age. He got a job as an army surgeon and was sent to the Indies — and there, by the river, he found some teeth and the top of a skull. Then he found some leg bones. From the shape of these he brilliantly proved that this creature had a brain halfway between an ape's and a man's and walked upright. He announced that he had found the *pithecanthropus erectus*.

Of course, there was a lot of wrangling. Some people said it was an ordinary ape. Some said it was an ordinary human idiot. Dr. Dubois said firmly that it was an ape-man who walked upright — and then one day he changed

Dubois dug up the remains of *pithecanthropus erectus*.

his mind and said it was an ape after all! But by then most people agreed with his first idea.

We have now found some more of this kind of creature, and he really must have been an upright ape-man—stupid, but perhaps able to speak, and with a big flat face and almost no forehead — who lived in the South Pacific while the early part of the Ice Age was going on.

In the 1920's and 1930's, in some caves **Who was** near what was **Peking Man?** called Chicken Bone Hill outside the city of Peking — now the capital of Red China — scientists dug up bits of the skulls and skeletons of about forty men, women and children.

They were about five feet tall and stocky. They stood straight. They seem to have been right-handed, with one side of their bodies slightly better developed than the other. Their faces were not quite as ape-like as the Java Man's, and their brains were a little bigger, but they lived about the same time as *pithecanthropus erectus* or a little later. What makes them tremendously interesting is that here at last we have found prehistoric man at home.

He was not a fellow you would care to visit for the weekend — although, surprisingly enough, he had fire and cooked some of his food, and was handy enough to make some quite useful tools by chipping and flaking pieces of stone. But either he used to have some rather unpleasant visitors or he was not fussy about his food, because the bones of wolves, wild dogs, foxes, hyenas and bears are mixed with his in the caves. There are also the bones of animals that do not live in caves, such as deer, sheep, buffaloes, bison, camels, rhinoceroses, a huge horse, ostriches and elephants. These must have been part of Peking Man's diet, for many of the bones have been split — so he could scoop out the marrow.

23

And there are another animal's bones on the pile — Peking Man's own bones, split for eating like the rest. He was a cannibal.

Just outside the German university town of Heidelberg there is a sandpit which, for nearly a century, has been a favorite spot for geologists and paleontologists, because its neat layers show the prehistoric events of Europe very simply. In 1907, a geologist named Schoetensack found what he had been seeking for twenty years — a piece of a man. It was a jawbone, probably about 400,000 years old — perhaps as old as *pithecanthropus erectus*.

Who was the first European?

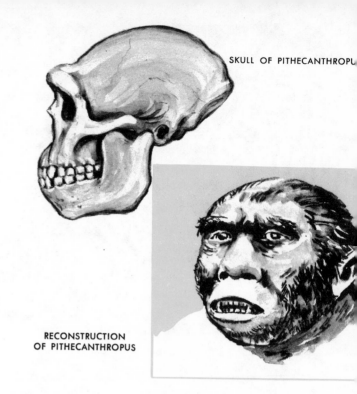

SKULL OF PITHECANTHROPU

RECONSTRUCTION OF PITHECANTHROPUS

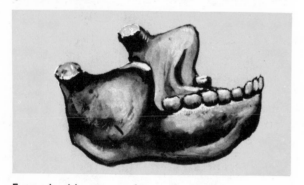

Europe's oldest trace of man: the Heidelberg jawbone.

It is the only trace of humanity found at the spot. It is the oldest trace of humanity in Europe. And it is still a mystery.

It is a jaw with all its teeth in place. The jaw is huge, chinless and rather ape-like, yet the teeth are of ordinary size and quite human.

Who was he — this flat-browed, big-headed, chinless stranger? Forty years of questioning have not brought an answer.

Before Darwin had told the world about his theories of evolution, there was already lying on a scientific society's shelves the skull of an early man — or rather an early woman — very much like what he said early humans must have been. But nobody seemed to notice it. It had been found in a cave on the Rock of Gibraltar in 1848 and given as a curiosity to the local scientific club. By the time it was sent to England, a skeleton of the same kind had been found in 1856 in a cave in the Neander Valley near the German city of Düsseldorf. So the name Neanderthal, instead of Gibraltar, was given to this kind of human being.

Who were the Neanderthals?

The Neanderthalers have been dug up in Spain, France, Belgium, Russia, Czechoslovakia, Yugoslavia and Italy. They are probably what you see in your mind's eye when you hear the words "cave man." This was a crude-faced creature with a sloping forehead, a long, wide nose, a large jaw and almost no chin. He slouched. He had big shoulders

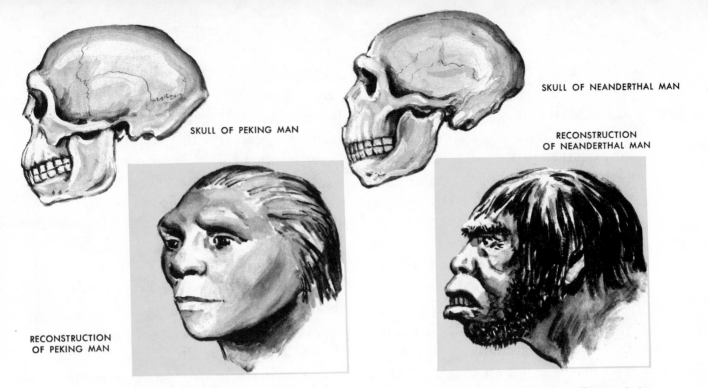

SKULL OF PEKING MAN

SKULL OF NEANDERTHAL MAN

RECONSTRUCTION
OF NEANDERTHAL MAN

RECONSTRUCTION
OF PEKING MAN

and short legs. He was a rugged fellow. He had to be. He lived in Europe in the Ice Age, 75,000 years ago. He was the man we saw in the forest in the first chapter. And by the way — he had a brain that was bigger than ours.

After Neanderthal Man was discovered, scientists soon got the idea that he was not our direct ancestor. Perhaps they hated the thought of having such a roughneck for a forefather. This fellow, they said, was another kind of man — a kind of evolutionary mistake. While Real Man, with his high forehead and fine jaw, was evolving quietly, the brawling Neanderthalers came along and bullied their way across Europe. Because they were strong, they won out during the harsh Ice Age. Because they were stupid, they lost in the end.

It was a good story. It seemed quite a clever way to explain the strange fact that there were some men from *before* Neanderthal times who in some ways looked less like apes and more like us.

But in 1931 and 1932, some American and English scientists found two adjoining caves on Mount Carmel in Palestine — now Israel — which contained the remains of a dozen people, along with their stone tools. The bones from one cave—Mugharet es Skhul, the Cave of the Young Goats—were a mixture of Modern and Neanderthal, mostly Modern, while some of the bones from next door were very Neanderthal. The more the scientists studied these finds, the more it seemed that Moderns and Neanderthalers had married each other and had children who had children. This was a very startling idea. Because the geneticists say definitely that this could not have happened if the Neanderthals were really on a different evolutionary path.

So the picture we now have of our Ice Age ancestors is this: Most scientists think that up to 150,000 years ago or so, there was one and only one basic kind of man. He was spread out over Europe, Asia, the South Pacific and Africa. Of course, there are some pretty noticeable differences between the people in those places — just as there are today. We can easily tell the difference between, say, the peoples of Scandinavia, the Soviet Union, the Mideast, the Far East, Africa, and Latin America. Many characteristics will often identify an ethnic or national background.

Then the terrible cold of the last glacier began to close in on Europe. A lot of the various tribes got out, going to places like Palestine. But a few were caught in Western Europe, surrounded by water and ice and freezing open plains. These diehard Europeans developed a special rugged build and appearance which was just an exaggeration of what they had started with — they were the Neanderthalers. When the glacier moved back a little, and they were finally able to reach the rest of the world, they mixed with the rest of mankind.

Sometimes they mixed a little more thoroughly with other people than they probably wanted to — some workers in a stone-quarry, in the section of southwestern Europe which is now called Yugoslavia, discovered some Neanderthal bones neatly split for eating. But just as often, no doubt, the Neanderthalers married with the other peoples, and soon lost their identity.

Here and there in Europe, perhaps as early as the middle of the Ice Age, there were a few breeds of men who looked much more modern than the tough Neanderthalers. A girl of twenty was found in some gravel near the Thames River in England. She was in a layer that contained the bones of rhinoceroses and elephants, which were

Who were the first "modern" men?

supposed to have come up from Africa and roamed in England during the long warm spell between the second and third glaciers. Yet this very old young lady is practically like an English girl of today.

A cave at Fontéchevade in France has yielded skulls similar to those of modern Frenchmen. Yet they were in with the bones of certain types of deer, tortoises and rhinoceroses that are supposed to belong to the warm period between the third and fourth glaciers.

As the Ice Age drew near its end, many interesting new types of people seem to have moved into what had been Neanderthal territory. The most famous is the Old Man of Cro-Magnon, found with four other skeletons in the Cro-Magnon cave in south central France. This man is typical of one of the two main kinds of people who were cropping up everywhere 15,000 years ago. He is a

little over five feet six inches tall, and he has a splendid big head — it held about ten percent more brains than the average European has today — with a high forehead and a good strong chin. The Cro-Magnon people looked a lot like modern Swedes and Norwegians.

The other main type of Late Ice Age people is called the Combe-Capelle type, also discovered in south central France. These were shorter folk than the Cro-Magnons, and they had big eyebrow-ridges and jaws — though not nearly as big as the Neanderthalers' — but their foreheads and chins were almost similar to our own.

Up to a few years ago, many people believed that we descended from the Cro-Magnons and only from the Cro-Magnons. They believed this mainly because they wanted to — the Cro-Magnons were the best-looking of all prehistoric men. Now we know that the Combe-Capelle and many other people were also mixed up in our ancestry.

At this point in our story we have, in fact, come so close to home that it is infuriating not to know more about all these people and what became of them. Europe and Asia and the Near East (that vital spot where so much of human history has started) were soon to be the scene of huge battles and far wanderings, of brilliant inventions and ignorant destructions, of mass disappearances and silent arrivals.

Did these cave-dwellers set out during the great thaw of 15,000 years ago and carry the sound of the human voice and the smoke of the campfire and the deadly cleverness of human fingers into the ancient wilderness? Did they meet older and simpler peoples on the way and slaughter the men and drag the frightened women and children along on their endless march? Did they become the fathers of new breeds of men, mixing the designs stored in their twists of nucleic acid with the mutations from hundreds of distant caves and rock-shelters?

Or did they stay in Europe? Or did some other breed of men, from some corner of the world which we have not explored, break in upon them and hunt them from valley to valley, as the white men broke in on the American Indians and hunted them, until only a handful were left in out-of-the-way forests?

Down on the French Riviera is the little principality of Monaco, famous for its gambling casino and its lovely Amer-

Were the early Europeans white men?

The cave-dwelling Cro-Magnons had to kill or drive away uninvited guests.

27

ican princess. Here, sixty years ago, in a cave called the Grotto of the Children, were found the bones of the lady known to anthropologists as the Widow of Grimaldi, along with her teenage son. They are a little like the Cro-Magnons, but there are some interesting things about them. No one, of course, can tell from a man's bones what color his skin was. But many physical anthropologists are convinced from the shape of the face and the length of the shins and forearms that here, on the north coast of the Mediterranean Sea, we have found two of the ancestors of the modern Negroes of Africa. Some even think they come from the time when the Africans were beginning to develop into a special kind of people.

And, once again in south central France, we have the famous Chancelade skeleton — the bones of a short, sturdy man of about sixty. He looks very much like an Eskimo, and a few scientists actually think he was an ancestor of the Eskimos, but even though we know nothing about the Eskimos until they suddenly appear about 2000 B.C., this is rather hard to believe. A famous anthropologist named Hooton said Chancelade man might have looked that way because his food was tough, like the tough fish that develops the Eskimo's jaws. Whoever these strangers were, it certainly was at this time that the hunters, forming themselves into bands and prowling the world for meat, began to divide into the races we know today.

The word "race" is a deadly word. A

What is a race?

few decades ago, six million Jewish people were murdered at the orders of the madman Hitler because he thought he belonged to a "master race" and his helpless victims belonged to a "lower race." The word "race" is dangerous because it is used with many different meanings, and most of them are cruel nonsense.

To the scientist — to the geneticist and the anthropologist — there is only one proper meaning: A race is a group of people who have had the same ancestors in recent times and whose bodies look pretty much alike. By bodies the scientists mean people's skin, hair, eyes, teeth, bones, blood cells and things like that — but not people's minds.

Scientists have studied people's minds very carefully. The nucleic acids that contain the master plan of a human being will sometimes decide whether he has a clever brain or a stupid brain, but they have nothing to say about what ideas there will be in that brain. Suppose we took an Eskimo baby to the South Sea Islands and raised him as a South Sea Islander. He would grow up looking like an Eskimo — short, with a wide, flat face, eyes with the slanting fold of skin over the corners, and straight black hair — not like a tall, brown-haired Tahitian. But he would think like a Tahitian. He would love the big round fruit of the breadfruit tree, while seal blubber would make him feel sick to his stomach. He would think that a loincloth made of pounded tree-bark was the only proper thing for a man to wear, and if we showed him a picture of his own father dressed in a fur parka, he would wonder who this strange, primitive creature could be.

There are as many different types of

Why did races evolve?

human bodies as there are kinds of places where humans live. The differences are astonishing. There are the almost blue-black Papuans of the South Pacific and the pale pink Northern Europeans. There are the fat Eskimos in Greenland and the skinny Bushmen of the Kalahari Desert in southern Africa. There are the Watusi Negroes of Africa, seven feet tall, and the Pygmies of Africa, four feet tall. And all go back to the same prehistoric ancestors.

While we still do not know very much about why such differences came about, we have discovered several fascinating facts. They all point to the same thing: All these race differences are ways in which men have become *specialists* in living in certain kinds of places.

Take skin color, for instance. There are

Why are some races dark-skinned?

three kinds of skin: a pinkish - white kind, which gets badly "burned" rather than "tanned" by sunlight; a chocolate-brown or black kind, which is not hurt by the fiercest sunlight; and a change-able kind — it may look white or olive or reddish or brownish — which turns tanner or paler according to how much sunlight touches it, and this last is the kind of skin which most of mankind has.

Sunlight contains ultra-violet rays

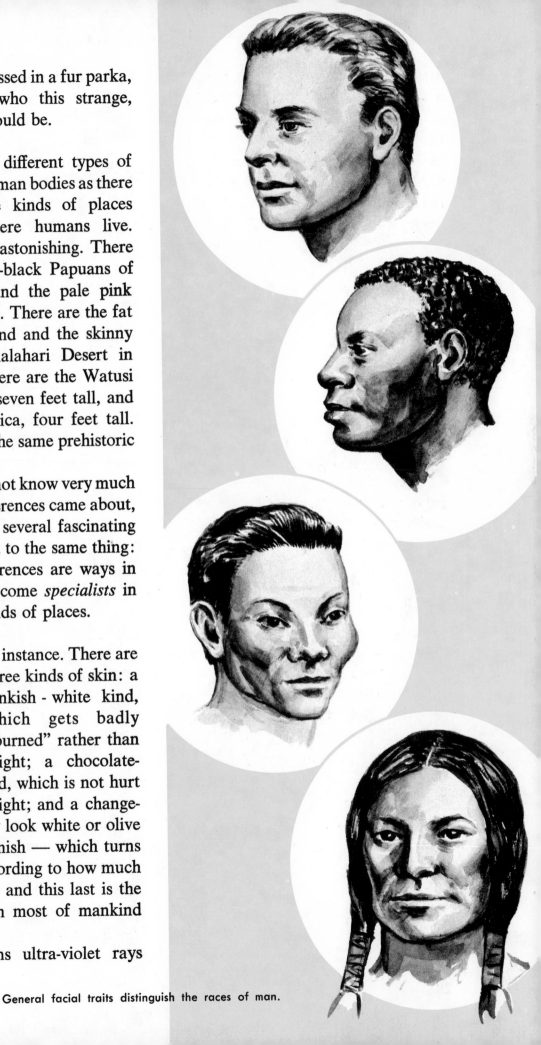

General facial traits distinguish the races of man.

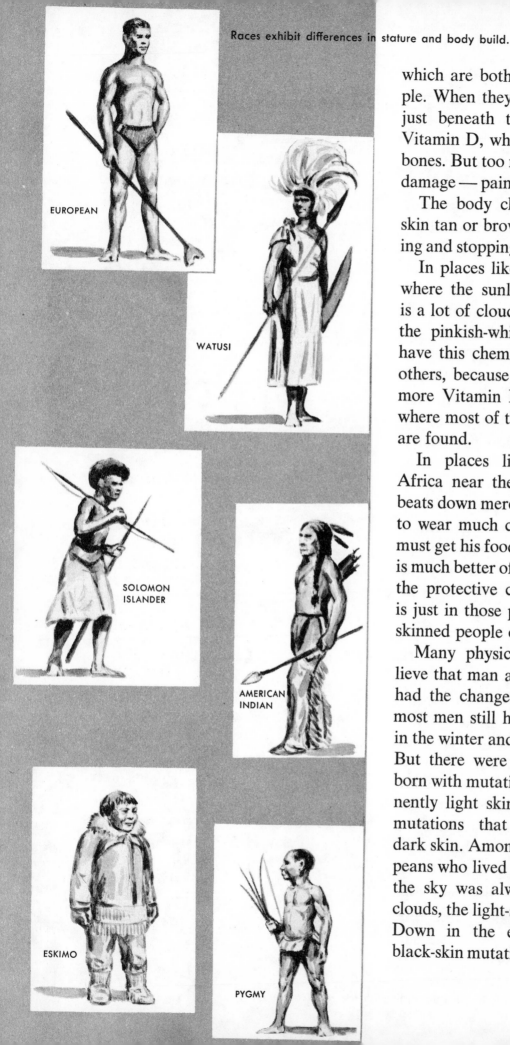

Races exhibit differences in stature and body build.

EUROPEAN

WATUSI

SOLOMON ISLANDER

AMERICAN INDIAN

ESKIMO

PYGMY

which are both good and bad for people. When they "irradiate" certain fats just beneath the skin, they produce Vitamin D, which is important for our bones. But too much sunlight can cause damage — painful sores and sunstroke.

The body chemical that colors the skin tan or brown has a way of absorbing and stopping ultra-violet rays.

In places like northwestern Europe, where the sunlight is weak and there is a lot of cloudy weather, people with the pinkish-white skin that does not have this chemical are better off than others, because their bodies can make more Vitamin D. And that is exactly where most of the pinkish-white people are found.

In places like the grasslands of Africa near the equator, the sunlight beats down mercilessly, and it is too hot to wear much clothing. A hunter who must get his food under that blazing sky is much better off if his skin is filled with the protective coloring-matter. And it is just in those places that the darkest-skinned people of the world are found.

Many physical anthropologists believe that man as he originally evolved had the changeable kind of skin that most men still have, which gets lighter in the winter and darker in the summer. But there were always some children born with mutations that caused permanently light skin and some born with mutations that caused permanently dark skin. Among the prehistoric Europeans who lived near the glacier, where the sky was always filled with snow-clouds, the light-skin mutation won out. Down in the equatorial plains, the black-skin mutation won.

The natural shape of a soap bubble is

Why are some races pudgy? round. That is because a sphere is the shape, which, as the mathematicians say, "has the least surface for a given volume." In other words, there is a certain amount of air in the bubble, and the soapy skin has to go around the outside of it, but since the skin is always trying to shrink, the air gets squeezed into the shape that needs the smallest outside skin or surface. A long, thin, cigar-shaped bubble would take much more soap-skin to hold the same amount of air. And *that* is why the Eskimos, for instance, look the way they do.

The Eskimos live in the icy north, on the edge of what is left of the Ice Age glacier. Many of them live in igloos, huts built out of blocks of ice. Even though they are wrapped in furs, they are never really warm. So their race has specialized in cold-weather living.

They are very round people, so they have room in their bodies for plenty of fat, which helps to hold in the body-heat and also helps them to live through the terrible weeks when seal or fish are scarce; and at the same time they do not have so much skin-surface to be cooled by the freezing air.

Their faces work the same way. Some physical anthropologists say that if you were to sit down and redesign your own face to protect it against the cold, you would end up with an Eskimo face. The slanting folds of skin around the eyes protect them from frosty air as well as from blinding reflections off the white snow. The flat brows and fat cheeks protect the delicate sinuses from cold. The

wide, big cheek bones shield both eyes and nose. Above all, the flat face keeps most of the features close to its round surface, instead of having them stick out where they can get frostbitten.

The Eskimos have stubby legs and arms. The Watusi Negroes of Africa, the tallest men on earth, have the longest and lankiest legs and arms. For their problem is the opposite of the Eskimos — they have to have a lot of skin surface to keep their bodies cool. You have noticed, of course, that when you wet your skin, even with warm water, it quickly begins to feel cool; evaporation cools. And this is why you sweat when you are overheated — it is your body's emergency cooling system. Now, a long, thin shape has a great deal of surface considering the amount of material inside; and if a man's legs and arms are lanky, his sweat-cooled skin can do the most efficient work in drawing off the heat from his blood-vessels, and thus cool the whole body.

A scientist, like any other man, is proud

Are some races smarter? of his own kind of people. But he is more proud of being honest. And so scientists who have studied other races of men — they are called *ethnologists,* which is Greek for "talkers about nations" — have usually reported that no matter where you go in the world and no matter what the people look like, there are some stupid ones and some clever ones and most are about the same.

This is probably because good brains help a man stay alive in any part of the world, so no group has evolved much

31

The Yahgan Indians of Tierra del Fuego, discovered by Captain Cook in 1774, did not develop beyond a primitive existence. Yet more than 2,000 years earlier, in Guatemala and Yucatán, the Mayan Indians already had a flourishing civilization. Above: a Yahgan hut; left and below: a Mayan palace, Yucatan ornaments.

faster or further than others, at least above the neck. Here and there, a band of prehistoric men may have wandered into some desolate part of the world where there is not much a man can do to make himself safer or healthier. For example, the natives of Tierra del Fuego at the southernmost tip of South America might well have been less smart than the other Indians to the north, even though they must have come from the same ancestors. And this could have been because the climate was so cold and harsh, and the things a man could use to make his life easier were so scarce, that the people who stayed alive the longest were the dull ones who could stand discomfort.

Always remember this: Men are men. There are no men now alive who are "nearer to the apes" than others.

32

Man's Works

The town of Abbeville lies near the northern coast of France, where the River Somme flows out into the English Channel. In the year 1830, Jacques Boucher de Crévecoeur de Perthes held the job of customs official in the town. He was supposed to inspect the cargoes of all the ships that sailed into the river mouth and make sure that the taxes were paid. It was not a hard job, so Boucher de Perthes had time to read about geology and to write stories and plays and books on government problems.

What were the first traces of early man?

One day, as he was taking his afternoon walk along the road that followed the river bank, he came upon some workmen. He stood watching them, the skirts of his greatcoat flapping in the damp sea breeze. Suddenly his eye caught a strangely shaped stone in the gravel river bank where they were digging. He walked over and picked it up. And modern man discovered his prehistoric ancestors.

It was a flint pebble shaped like a pear, and the narrower end had been chipped away to form a jagged point. The chipping could not have been accidental. A man must have done it.

Boucher de Perthes looked down at the layers of packed-down gravel, hundreds and hundreds of centuries old, where the stone had been buried, and asked himself: "But what man *could* have done this?" For in those days no one thought man had been on the earth for more than 6,000 years. He shifted the stone in his hand so that the round end nestled in his palm, and in his mind's eye he saw not his own smooth white fingers holding an interesting pebble, but the hairy fist of some man of incredibly ancient times clutching a sharp stone claw as he chopped at a savage enemy.

But although Boucher de Perthes had the imaginative mind of a writer of stories when he looked at the fist-axe, he also had the cautious mind of a government official. He said nothing. He came to the river road during his spare time and dug in the gravel. Where the flint tool had been lying, he found the bones of elephants and rhinoceroses! A great new story of prehistoric Europe formed in his mind, but still he said nothing.

It was not until sixteen years later that he sat down to write his book proving that there had been men on earth — tool-using men — fifty or a hundred thousand years before. And it was fifteen years more before the last scoffing professor was convinced. And by that

Abbevillian bifaces: one of man's early stone tools.

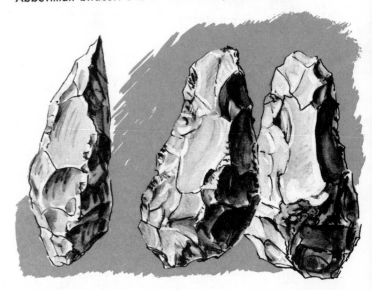

time Darwin had written his great book and the skulls of prehistoric men had been found.

Stand in front of the mirror. Look. You are a wonderfully designed animal. You are standing on your hind legs, and that means that your front limbs are free to fight or to point or to lift things. They do not have to help you move around, as a horse's or a tiger's do.

What is a tool?

Lift your arm. Look. This forelimb of yours is a powerful instrument. It has a ball-and-socket joint at the shoulder. It has a strong folding joint at the elbow. It has a turning joint at the wrist. It has a very clever system of muscle-cables inside its skin to control this useful apparatus. You can move heavy things easily.

Hold out your hand. Look. Each of your fingers bends in three places. You can turn your thumb so that it lies right across the palm of your hand. You can grip big things and little things. You can hold them tightly or firmly. You can twist, turn, pull, push or throw things of any shape. Backing up the tips of your fingers are the tough flat nails. They make the ends of your fingers stiff enough to hold things without your having skin so coarse and hard that you could not do delicate work. Your hand is a tool that makes it possible for you to have other tools.

Yet other animals are almost as well designed as you are. Apes can walk on their hind legs, though they normally get a little help from their hands. They can cross their thumbs over, and they can hold and move things in their

AXE

HARPOON

fingers. But they do not use tools. Their brains lack something.

When your hairy ancestor picked up a sharp stone to scrape something or a heavy stone to hammer something, it was a tremendous idea. *He was making an addition to his body. His mind was giving his body a new power over the world around him.*

And when he could not find the right stone, and instead of poking in the gravel all day for what he wanted, he just picked up another stone and chipped the first stone into the right shape, it was an even more tremendous idea. *He was changing the world around him to fit himself. His mind gave him a picture of something good that did not exist yet and he made it exist.*

The ordinary animal needs certain things — certain foods, certain shelter, a certain climate. When the things

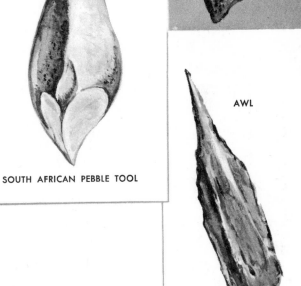
Where workmen were dredging a river bank, Boucher de Perthes dug up animal bones and tools of early man.

HAND AXE

SOUTH AFRICAN PEBBLE TOOL

AWL

around him are not what he needs, he goes somewhere else. Birds and bees build nests. Spiders make webs. Beavers build dams. But if they do not have the right tree or corner or stream, they cannot design a new kind of nest or web or dam, and they cannot change the tree or corner or stream that is there. They have to go away.

But when a man first changed the shape of a stone, he became the first animal that said: "World, we don't suit each other, you and I — and *you're* going to change!"

And from that moment on, man was surely going to have weapons, which were killing-tools.

And fire, which changed food and climate for him.

And clothing, which was portable shelter.

And art, which was a way his mind

SPEARHEAD

told itself about the things he wanted, but did not have yet.

And language, which started as a way of pointing at things and became a way his mind told other minds about things that were not around for him to point at.

And, much later, herds of animals and fields full of crops, which were man's way of saying to all other living things: "I chose *you* to live in this world with me and for me, and *you others* I don't want."

What were the first tools? If one of our man-ape ancestors needed a heavy stone to hammer something or a sharp stone to scrape something, he poked around until he found one, and when he finished with it he would throw it away. He had no pockets, because he had no clothes.

And when the ape-man changed the shape of a stone to make it more useful, he naturally chose the stone that needed the least work done on it. And the work he did on it by chipping or splitting was so crude that we usually cannot tell it from accidental chipping or splitting.

Museums are full of what are called *eoliths* — Greek for "dawn stones" — which are supposed to be these earliest work tools. But it is hard to see the human workmanship in most of them.

MORTAR

How old are the earliest tools? The earliest tools we have found that show pretty definite signs of having been worked on by men seem to be older than any of the men we have found. They have

been dug up in Africa, both in the south and in the north of that mysterious continent. Some of them are more than a half-million years old.

They are split pebbles larger than your fist, with one side chipped to make a sort of sharp edge. As the first glacier sent the ape-men roaming over the wildernesses of the Old World between the Ice and the fiery desert, these "pebble tools" must have spread from one wandering band to another.

Then, over thousands and thousands of years, the bands in the west — in Europe and Africa and Central Asia — began to improve their crude implements. The bands of the east — in what is now China and the South Sea Islands — learned to improve theirs, too, but in a different way.

PIERCER

NEEDLES

Stone Age man chipped pieces from a chunk of flint to make a fist-axe.

Nobody knows when primitive man succeeded in making fire, but it was a giant step.

Around the time of the second glacier,

How were "fist-axes" made? perhaps 300,000 to 400,000 years ago, word spread among the western peoples of an important invention. It was the "fist-axe" — though probably the tool was used for prying and picking and scraping as much as for chopping. The technical name for it is "core-biface," because when prehistoric man made it by chipping away at a pear-shaped stone to form an edge or point, he kept the big stone or "core" and threw the chips away — and he chipped at both sides or "faces" of it.

This was the tool that Boucher de Perthes found in the gravel of the Somme River. Many like it have been found all over Africa, Europe and Central Asia. Who used them? We do not

know. We have never found them together with their owners — at least, not until we come to the handsome core-bifaces that were still being made hundreds of thousands of years later.

One day, while the western tribes were

How are "flake tools" made? still just learning how to make core-bifaces, a great scientific genius was sitting on a gravel heap making himself a large fist-axe. He struck too hard with his hammer-stone, and instead of the neat little chip he wanted to take off, a wide, flat flake fell to the ground. He picked it up and looked at it. He felt its sharp edge and his eyes under the heavy brow-ridges narrowed. He was thinking about stones in a new way. He tried to remember how he had held the core-stone and the hammer-stone, and he struck again. An ordinary chip fell off. Again. A fair-sized flake. Again. A beautiful thin, sharp tool.

Soon the news was passed from tribe to tribe that if you could find good core-stones you could make many handfuls of tools from one stone, and make them quickly.

It used to be thought that the people who made core-bifaces and the people who made flake tools were different kinds of men. Some scientists even had visions of great wars fought all over the west between core-bifaces and flakers, and a few even dreamed of Neanderthal villains with jagged little flakes fighting Cro-Magnon heroes carrying well-made core-bifaces. Others argued that the same men probably had both kinds of tools. After all, we have many kinds of tools and we do not have wars between Wrench Tribes, Pliers Tribes, Razor Tribes and Screwdriver Tribes. In 1906, a Frenchman digging near the Somme River — the same river where prehistoric tools were first found — came upon a gravel pit which had been used as an open-air workshop. And here some very early men had worked side by side making core-bifaces and flake-tools.

For untold centuries, these two kinds of stones were the tool-kit and armory of the west.

38

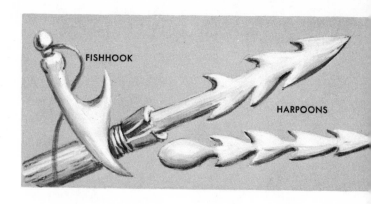

Of all the early stone tools, the only

What tools did Peking Man use?

ones that have been found along with their owners are the tools with Peking Man at Chicken Bone Mountain. They are also the only early ones found in a cave. The rest were all found out in the open.

These eastern tools are quite different from the tools used in Europe. They are what are called "chopper-chopping tools." Some are wide scrapers. Some are heavy cleavers. Some have points. But big or small, wide or pointed, they are made like "hand adzes." An adze is a little different from an axe. The cutting edge of an axe is sharpened on both faces; the edge of an adze is chipped away on one face only. No doubt they were useful in splitting bones during feasts.

An ax is shaped like this:

An adze is shaped like this.

For two or three thousand centuries,

What did man invent in the Ice Age?

while the ice closed in and drew back again and again, man produced no

really new ideas. The old ways of mak-

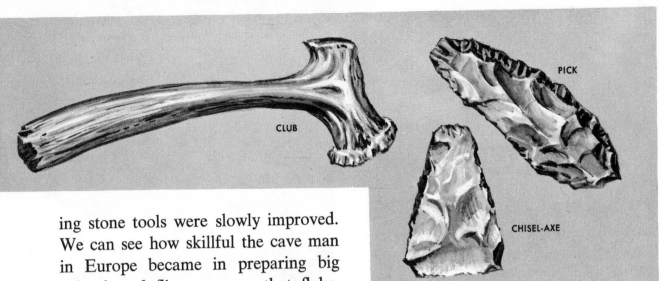

CLUB

PICK

CHISEL-AXE

ing stone tools were slowly improved. We can see how skillful the cave man in Europe became in preparing big cake-shaped flint cores so that flake-tool after flake-tool could be whacked off with swift, clean blows. The core-bifaces begin to be flat and even-shaped and sharp.

Then, in the warm spell before the last glacier, there was a great stirring among the minds of the prehistoric men of Europe. By the time the mountains of ice came grinding down, men had set up tribe-households in caves. They began to make tools out of new materials, and their stone tools took new forms. During the endless winter, they invented throwing-sticks to help their arms hurl their spears farther. They tied strips of animal hide together to make ropes, and attached bone har-

poons to them with cleverly carved barbs to catch in the flesh of animals. They made bows and arrows, and some of their arrows had bone tips. Their stone spear-points and arrowheads were as fine as laurel leaves. They learned to use long cone-shaped flint cores from which they could flake off knife-blades and chisels. As the Ice Age came to an end, the men who followed the glaciers up from the Mediterranean Sea were making very small, delicately-worked stone arrowheads and tools which we call *microliths* (Greek for "tiny stones").

Story of the Cave Man Paintings

He was afraid. He squatted in the yellow dancing firelight next to the other young men of the cave, and he hoped they would not see how his lips and his fingers were shaking. For the time had again come when he must go

down into The Darkness, down into the hungry belly of the earth.

For many days now — ever since this moon was born — the hunting had been bad, and the people of the cave were weak from lack of food. Yesterday an old woman and a young girl had died. The cunning old hunters and the strong young hunters went out early every day, and came back late — with nothing but their dry, clean spears and knives. All the berries and nuts had long ago been stripped from the branches. There were two children who were already too weak to walk, and an old man who once was wise and merry but who now slept all day and all night.

The men of the cave met together and decided. Some said this moon was a Moon of Weakness, and the hunters would have no power over the animals until the moon grew fat and thin and died, and a new, thin sliver of moon was born in the sky. But others said that the Magic of the cave was all used up, and more Magic must be made. Then the first ones said that Magic could do nothing under a Moon of Weakness, and the new Magic must be made at the birth of

Led by a chanting Healer, the cave men danced as a means of attaining power over animals they hunted.

Cave man artists sought power over the animals which they depicted in color on the cave walls.

the new moon. But the others said that the people of the cave could not wait, for the new moon would not be born for two-handfuls-and-three-more-fingers of days. And so the decision was that the Healer would dance tonight and the chosen men — an old man and a young man — would go down into the belly of the earth, away from the sight of the Moon of Weakness, and make the Magic of Power.

And he was the chosen young man. He licked his dry lips.

Next to him, his younger brother was preparing for tomorrow's great hunt. He was making a new spear-thrower. He had taken one of the great antlers he and his father had saved from many hunts, and had broken off all the points until he had a fine straight piece of horn. Now he was smoothing it with a beautiful flint blade their father had just made. Carefully the boy formed it, a thin rod as long as his forearm, with a little groove and a notch that turned the end of it into a hook. Throwers were hard to use — you held the thrower with three fingers of your hand, the hook pointed back past your shoulder. You laid the spear along the thrower, with the blunt end nestling back against the hook and the spearhead forward, while you held the middle of the spear-shaft with the other two fingers of your throwing hand. Then a swift, whipping throw — with the extra reach that the thrower gave your arm — and the spear whistled forward faster than any man's arm alone could have hurled it. It was hard, but young as little brother was, he was making a good thrower, and he could use it well.

Their father was making spear points. The old man had the Rain Sickness in his fingers, and the swollen knuckles did not bend well any more. Yet the wisdom of many years was still in his hands, and he could make the terrible weapons he could not use. He had a large chunk of flint that he had carefully chipped down into a cone shape — this was the Mother of Blades. Against it he held the tip of a little punch made of bone, and whacked it with the hammer-stone, the Father of Blades. And so keen was the old man's eye and so great was the cunning of his hands that each whack chipped off a flat blade with the lovely, deadly-sharp edges that only good flint could give.

Whack! Whack! Whack! Three perfect blades. They would make good knives to cut meat. With a little chipping, they would make scrapers to clean the animal hides, or punches to sew the hides into clothing. But tonight the people had no meat and no furs — they still had to get them. So the old man began to chip at the beautiful blades, taking off tiny flakes until he had fashioned a spearhead shaped like

Early man scraped the tough, rough hides of animals with stone implements to soften the skins which clothed him.

a leaf, a leaf of death, a leaf of power.

The young man looked from his busy brother to his busy father, and then looked down at the strange tools beside his own feet: The little bone pot, made of rabbit's skull, filled with black soot from the fire; the stone pots with lumps of sun-dried red clay and yellow clay in them; the little strip of hide; the skull-bowls of water; and the unlit lamps composed of three shallow stone basins, with wicks made of the braided hair of young girls, filled with the last animal fat that the people of the cave had. (There had been five lamps, but a hungry child had drunk the fat from two of them.) These were his tools, the tools of the Magic of Power.

Slowly and with unsteady hands, he began to crush the colored clay into powder, using a round pebble. The powder must be fine, must be perfect. He was so absorbed in his task that he did not notice when the sounds of the stone-chipping and wood-scraping died down and the talking stopped and a hush fell over the people of the cave. But he heard the hoarse voice of the Healer say, "Come!" and he stood up. The older chosen man helped him to pour and mix the water into the pots of black, red and yellow powder, and to light two of the lamps at the fire. He carried one lighted lamp and the black pot. The Healer carried the other lighted lamp and the old red pot. The young man carried the unlit lamp and the yellow pot, along with the strips of hide. They turned from the fire, which was at the cave entrance, and walked into the darkness at the back of the cave.

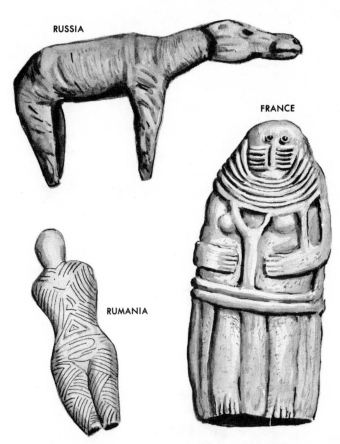

RUSSIA

FRANCE

RUMANIA

Figures, found in Europe, made by Stone Age men.

The men of the cave followed a little way behind, their hands full of spears and spear-throwers and stone knives. The silent procession passed into the deepest shadows, and stooped, one by one, to go into the small black hole in the wall of the cave.

The sputtering lamps cast a faint, shaky glow on the sides of the narrow passage. It was cold, but it was not the cold that made the young man's teeth chatter as he followed the Healer and the old man.

Behind him, there were groans and mumblings of fright from some of the men, and fierce whispers to be quiet from others. Was there a snake's hiss?

Down they went, into the dim vault of another cavern, where the two crackling braids of hair in the bowls of ani-

One of the most beautiful examples of early cave man paintings was found in southwestern France at Lascaux Cave.

A cave wall frequently shows stenciled hands, sometimes even mutilated as the cave man's hand might have been.

mal fat showed the bones of a bear and several smaller animals. A rat scurried almost under their feet and ran squeaking into the darkness. They came to another passage-entrance, and suddenly one of the men threw down his weapons and began to run the way they had come. "Come back!" someone cried, and the whole group called, "Come back! Come back!" But it was not necessary. The frightened man took ten steps into the awful shadows, stopped, turned, and ran back to catch up with the disappearing glow of the two lamps. Others had picked up his weapons before the light was gone.

At last they came to the place. The men piled their weapons in the center of the dark cave, calling each by name. Their eyeballs gleamed yellow in the lamplight as they looked toward the Healer. From among the spears, he drew a noble pair of deer antlers attached to a strip of deerhide and quickly tied them to his head.

He began his chant, calling the animals of the forest by their Own Names, and boasting loudly of the Power of the people of the cave and the Power of the weapons over all animals.

Meanwhile, some of the hunters ran to the wall of the cavern and held their

right hands flat against it. The old chosen man and the young chosen man hastily dipped the strips of fur into the paint-bowls and traced the outlines of the hands on the stone, some in red, some in black, some in yellow. There were great, strong, young hands. There were old hands knotted with the Rain Sickness. There were hands with two or even three fingers missing. Swiftly they were painted on the wall, and then the hunters gathered near the old man who, holding one lamp aloft, led them into the passages through which they had come.

They stumbled in their hurry, for there was not much grease left in their lamp-bowl, and if the flame died out before they reached the outer cave, they might wander in the blackness into a wrong passage and be lost, swallowed in the earth's belly.

The young man and the Healer were left alone.

The Healer danced, calling more and more wildly on the animals to submit to the Power of man. Name after name he shouted, names of animals, names of the winds, names of weapons, the secret words of Power.

And the young man painted. First he drew a great bison, proud in its huge strength, with the rich folds of fat and muscle hanging down between its thin, short forelegs, and the tail lashing. A rub of black and a rub of yellow, quickly made with the little fur strips — and the brown of the big beast's fur was properly caught on the cave wall. The small red-rimmed eyes with the staring black dots in the center — and the animal's fierce temper was caught.

"Submit! Submit!" chanted the Healer, calling the bison by name. "The Power is man's!"

The young man forgot to tremble with fear. He forgot to hurry. He forgot to watch the sputtering lamp on the floor by his feet, to see when it was burning low and the other lamp must be lighted. He was painting the proudest and strongest of all bisons, catching its living strength and its terrible spirit on the wall of the cave.

It was the Healer who stopped his chant and, just in time, leaped to the lamp as the flame started to sink and grow dim. If the new lamp was not lighted from the old, they would be lost forever. Feverishly, he held the hair-wick of the unlighted lamp to the dying flame. It caught, smoked, and went out, caught again, smoked, and went out. "Power of Fire! Power of Fire!" shrieked the Healer, and called the secret name of the Sun Itself. Just as the old lamp died, the tiny flame of the new one hung for a moment on a bubble of the fat, smoked dangerously, and then started to grow bright.

The Healer drew off his deerskin breech-clout and his tiger-skin cape and began to pile the weapons in them,

throwing the used-up lamp onto one pile and tying it up in a bundle. "Come! Come now!" he said harshly.

But the young man had more work to do. He had begun to paint a deer. "Dance!" he said in a low voice. "Sing, dance! The people are dying of hunger. The Magic must be strong!" His hand, holding the soot-black fur, swept over the wall and traced the strong line of the animal's flanks as it leaped in the air. His fingers dipped another fur-strip in the red pot and began the coloring and shading of the muscles in the neck and legs. There was an old, dried painting of a mammoth in the way, left by some earlier people of the cave. The young man painted over it as if it were not there.

The Healer's chant was quick and all the wildness had gone out of it, and soon he called, "Come! Do you hear!"

The young man flung the empty paint pots into the second pile of weapons, tied it all up in the fur cape, and staggered as he lifted the huge bundle. He also slung the other bundle over his shoulder, held the lamp high, and led the way up through the darkness toward the campfire and the people waiting for the dawn and the hunt.

How Did Civilization Come to the Cave Men?

About 15,000 years ago, the last glacier (we hope) began its last retreat from Europe. By 10,000 B.C., the big hardy animals that lived at the edge of the cold — the mammoth and the woolly rhinoceros—had crashed away through the northern forests and were dying out. The reindeer were moving north. The forests were full of smaller, swifter animals. The seasons were different. The rising oceans poured into the lowlands, and England and Ireland turned into islands. The Forest People came out of their caves and built summer camps by the shores of lakes. They tamed the dog, but they did not know what a tremendous idea was wagging its tail at their very feet. They even forgot their beautiful art. As change followed change, they had to turn their minds to ingenious new hunting-weapons of wood and bone, and new tools, and new kinds of camps.

We have found a camp of the Forest People, wonderfully preserved in a great swamp in Denmark. It is the home of clever, practical people, but not people with great new ideas, not people who were inventing civilization. Europe, where man had done so much and learned so much, was now just an out-of-the-way place.

In the Middle East, in what is now **Where did civilization begin?** the Arab country of Iraq, flowed two mighty rivers, the Tigris and the Euphrates, bringing water and life in a great green streak across the harsh plains and hills. The streak bent over westward to the Syrian shore of the Mediterranean Sea, and southward to where the Biblical city of Jericho was later to stand. It was in this Fertile Crescent, as we now call it, that human civilization began ten thousand years ago.

On the slopes above the two rivers grew certain wild plants — wheat and barley. Certain wild animals — goats, pigs, sheep, horses, oxen and dogs — roamed the lower hills. Perhaps it was a hunter running with his dog who said: "If I can tame a dog — why not a goat, a horse, a sheep?" Or perhaps it was a mother, gathering the little kernels of wheat, who said: "Why, these are the seeds of the wheat plant! If I put them in the ground next to my shelter, the plant will grow there and I will not have to walk so far."

Anyway, the enormous idea came into the minds of men. They became food *producers* instead of food *gatherers*. By 9000 B.C., they were planting and harvesting crops.

A man who goes from cave to cave or hut to hut, following the animals he

From a cave to the lake-dweller's hut was a big step.

Man became a food *producer* instead of a *gatherer*.

eats, does not build a good hut or home — he has no time, and anyway he will not use it for long. He has no breakable possessions and very little clothing, because he must always be ready to carry everything he owns.

But a man who grows crops and tends flocks knows he will stay in one place. He builds a good house and a barn or silo to store his grain. He gives his family work to do. He lives close to his neighbors so everyone can help with the planting and harvesting and the guarding of the sheep. He builds a village. By 8000 B.C. there were many villages.

There were water-springs in the hills above the slopes of the Fertile Crescent. Sometimes the two rivers raged out of control and carried away the homes and flocks and crops of the farmers. If the farmers could build earth walls, the waters could be sent only into fields that needed it, and if the farmers could dig ditches to let the water flow from the springs down to the dry fields, they

could plant crops back away from the river, where they would be safer. So irrigation was invented before 4000 B.C.

Men learned to mold clay into bowls and bake it. The bowls would have been too breakable for hunter families, but they were needed by farm families. Pottery had been invented by 5000 B.C.

The village grew into cities. Men exchanged their goods and traded. Money was invented. And the news of these great ideas traveled into Europe. By 3000 B.C., farming had spread to France and Spain.

Staying together in one place and helping each other, men found that they had to remember many things — who owned what, who owed what, how this must be done, how that could be prevented. To help them remember, they drew pictures. Instead of laboriously carving on hard bone or stone, they could scratch their pictures into soft clay and bake it hard. The pictures grew simpler and easier. People agreed on what a few quickly scratched lines would stand for, and before 3000 B.C., somewhere in the heart of the Fertile Crescent, writing was invented.

History had begun.